SIMPLIFY
AND LIVE THE GOOD LIFE

How to Be Really Wealthy
in All Areas of Life

BO SANCHEZ

OTHER BOOKS BY BO SANCHEZ

THE BOSS Series
Thank God He's Boss
You Can Make Your Life Beautiful
You Have the Power to Create Love

SIMPLIFY Series
Simplify and Live the Good Life
Simplify and Create Abundance

PRAYERBOOKS
Embraced
The Way of the Cross
Special Prayers for the Rosary

To the wonderful leaders of my little spiritual family —
you testify to me that God pampers me
with His very best.

6

SIMPLIFY
AND LIVE THE GOOD LIFE

SIMPLIFY
AND LIVE THE GOOD LIFE
Discover a Simple Path to Happiness

ISBN 971-91756-7-2

BO SANCHEZ

SIMPLIFY and Live the Good Life
Copyright © 2001 by Shepherd's Voice Publications, Inc.

Requests for information should be addressed to:
SHEPHERD'S VOICE Publications
#60 Chicago St., Cubao, Quezon City, Philippines 1109
Tel. No. (02) 411-7874 to 77
Fax No. 727-5615
e-mail: sale@shepherdsvoice.com.ph

Cover design by Noli Vicedo
Layout by Rey de Guzman

CONTENTS

PREFACE

The older I grow, the more clearly I perceive the dignity and winning beauty of simplicity in thought, conduct and speech: a desire to simplify all that is complicated and to treat everything with the greatest naturalness and clarity.
— Pope John XXIII, Journal of a Soul

My parents breathed simplicity.

Oxygen too, but that's pretty obvious.

Dad was an assistant vice president for a humongous company, yet I didn't "feel" like I was a rich man's kid. Because my parents made it a rule to live below their means. A millionaire's son rode a sleek Benz; I rode our 16-year old Toyota that sounded more like a drum and bugle band, with its cacophony of bangs, rattles and whams. An heir of the moneyed class was chauffeured to school, but as early as Grade III, I was taking the public jeepney — sitting, standing or swinging from its handrails like a flapping flag.

The wealthy dined on gourmet meals every day. But the culinary highlight of my whole week was when Mom bought Coke for our Sunday lunch — the only time we tasted the stuff. I'm not kidding.

Rich kids wore outfits from America, England and Paris. I wore clothes from Avenida, Escolta, and Pasay.[1]

The mansions of the rich and famous are veritable furniture showcases, complete with 16 Egyptian jars from the Nephertiti era. I learned that one of those monstrous flower vases was equal to the price of our entire house. But naturally, we too, had our own flower vases. If my archeological knowledge serves me right, they came from the Nescafé era.

Their estates have playrooms with life-size Barbies and Power Rangers. But the way I played with expensive toys was admiring them from the store shelf and using my imagination to the hilt. That way, I owned all the toys in the world.

You'll be shocked by what I'm going to tell you, but through all this, I never recall feeling deprived in any way.

Let me tell you why.

I remember my father coming home every night and we'd go jogging together — around our old car parked in the garage. (Dad says he wasn't vying for the Olympics anyway.) Then I'd sit on his lap and we'd talk about how to solve the problems of the universe. After dinner, we'd read the comic pages together. Tarzan was my favorite, until I reached puberty. From then on, it became Jane.

---

[1]*Local sites in Manila*

Almost every Saturday afternoon, it was father and son time. We'd walk to the shopping center and Dad would buy me a hotdog. Then we'd walk back home, bringing a little something for Mom, usually a chocolate bar. To add sentimental value to our token, I forced myself to take a few bites from it.

I guess being with Dad and Mom were all that my little boy's heart ever wanted.

And I got it, every single day.

✳✳✳

I believe that God chose to write the "map of happiness" on the ordinary parchment of *simplicity* – like a treasure map written on recycled brown paper. Consequently, many people ignore that map, and are attracted instead to the more glossy, loud, shiny maps around. But when they follow these others maps, they end up tired as a dog chasing its own tail.

I have a radical suggestion.

Simplify.

Simplify because you want to discover the depths of your soul.

Simplify because you want to start living *deliberately*.

Simplify because you want to love from an uncluttered heart.

Remember that simplicity is only the first step of the journey. Holding the treasure map, memorizing it, photocopying it a thousand times and keeping it safe in a vault won't make you claim the gold. You actually need to sail through oceans, climb peaks, cross valleys and explore caves.

Simplicity will point to you where and what and who the gold is in your life.

Once you know your gold, the game has just begun.

Will you *treasure* your gold?

My parents knew their gold: (1) each other, (2) their six children, and (3) their faith. They tried to live uncluttered lives so that they could have time for what was most important.

They didn't busy themselves buying a bigger house, because that would mean working harder to pay the monthly amortization, doing overtime work or taking a second job. Who would then go jogging with little Bo every night? Who would read Tarzan for him? They didn't burden themselves buying a BMW because that would mean laboring and worrying about installment bills. Besides, walking to the shopping center every Saturday afternoon with his son gave my dad his needed exercise, and made little Bo feel special.

One of the delights of my heart was seeing Dad and Mom in their bedroom at night, after our nightly family prayer. The lights were turned off, and I'd see the silhouette of my father seated on his old chair and mom standing behind him, gently massaging his shoulders. I'd hear them talk about what transpired during their day. Even as a child, I sensed their quiet pleasure at being together. My question today: Could they have done this rich ritual each night and nourished their marriage if they had been busy paying for designer outfits for themselves or their kids, or if they had been worrying about monthly bills for new hi-tech appliances?

I don't think so.

And I've made the choice: I don't want that kind of life either.

It is then my pleasure to take you now through the peaks and valleys of this journey towards happy simplicity.

LIVE FROM THE CORE OF YOUR BEING

It is not enough if you are busy.
The question is, What are you busy about?
—*Henry David Thoreau*

Happiness is not found outside of you. It doesn't come from cars, clothes, cash or Caribbean cruises. Happiness is found within.

But how can you find it if you don't have the *simplicity of time and space* to discover the most important things in your life? How can you search the depths of your soul if you are too busy impressing others, acquiring wealth, protecting your properties and paying your debts?

Simplicity is NOT about the externals either: living in a doghouse, eating in a Hepatitis joint, wearing rags.

The best definition of simplicity I have ever read comes from Janet Luhrs's book, *The Simple Living Guide.* There she says that **simplicity is living from the core of your being.**

I cannot agree more.

I believe that simplicity is having the time and space to embrace what is *most* important to you. It is having the leisure to cherish it, having the freedom to glory in it, and having the power to live by it.

Along the way, you'll discover that the most important things in life aren't things but the persons who have become part of our lives. But that's something you'll have to discover yourself.

Give up shallowness.

Live from the core of your being.

Action Plan

Get a notebook and begin a journal for this book. Write down your discoveries, insights, reflections and action plan for each chapter.

What is your *core*? What are the most important things in your life right now? Do you allow your core to direct and empower your daily decisions and actions?

LIVE ON LESS, AND DELIGHT IN IT MORE

There are two ways to get enough:
one is to continue to accumulate more and more.
The other is to desire less.
— G.K. Chesterton

Relish, taste and immerse yourself in the divine of the ordinary! Because if you develop the capacity to suck all the joy that life has to offer, you don't need expensive entertainment.

I'm not ashamed to say that looking through an open window and seeing clouds drift by is Class A entertainment for me. Doing that for just five minutes sets the tenor of my day.

Some take their pleasure from dining in classy restaurants, going on trips to Europe and owning the latest home theater equipment. I've chosen the simpler path: If I can simply be with my wife, or take a quiet stroll under a canopy of stars, or play with a child, or read a good book in my home, or laugh with friends over pizza, I consider myself richly blessed.

Focus on what you have, not on what you don't.
Because satisfaction doesn't come from getting what you want, but wanting what you already have.

I have learned the secret of being content in any and every situation, whether well fed or hungry, whether living in plenty or in want. I can do everything through him who gives me strength.
— *Philippians 4:12-13*

Think about it.

Action Plan
What do you have right now that you have been taking for granted? List down in your journal 50 blessings you enjoy today. Don't stop until you reach 50!

KNOW THAT HAPPINESS ISN'T ONLY FOR MILLIONAIRES

Whoever does not regard what he has as ample wealth is unhappy, though he be the master of the world.
—*Epicurus*

People think that happiness is expensive. If you look at the list below, they seem to be right!

Buffet lunch at Shangri-La Hotel	P800++
Wearing a pair of Ferragamo shoes	P16,000
Driving, or being driven, in a Jaguar	P22 million
Lying beside a pool in cool Polo shorts	P4,000
Checking the time on a Rolex	P300,000
Malling in a Lacoste shirt	P3,500
Seeing the glint of a one karat diamond ring (average)	P100,000+
Walking in a party in an elegant Armani suit	P150,000
Watching a movie from a personal home theater	P250,000
Cuddling up in a Marks and Spencers pajamas	P2,400

Daubing the scent of	
Estee Lauder perfume, small bottle	P2,000
Traveling "business class"	
instead of "tourist" (U.S. trip)	$2,000

There are people I know who don't think that happiness is expensive. But what they do is awesomely enriching. For them, happiness means:

Being quiet in prayer	
for 10 minutes each morning	P0.0
Giving a glass of water to	
the postman and garbage collector	P0.0
Laughing with friends	P0.0
Calling up their mothers	
and telling them they miss her	P5.00 per three mins.
Reading a good book (Borrow one!)	P0.0
Visiting a home for the elderly	
and listening to the stories of a *lola*	P0.0
Taking a quiet walk with a	
loved one while holding hands	P0.0
Choosing to sleep in until	
10:00 AM one Saturday morning	P0.0
Making popcorn and holding	
a songfest with the kids	P50.00
Giving roses from the market to	

a friend with an original poem   P35.00
Wrestling with an eight-year-old son,
and letting him win   P 0.0
Making love to your spouse   P 0.0

Know that happiness isn't only for millionaires.

Action Plan

What simple joys do you regularly have in your life similar to those mentioned above?

Make a list of other inexpensive pleasures you want to try. Take your calendar and schedule some of these activities in the coming week. If you don't do this, there's a big chance that you will forget about these not-so-urgent but very important "celebrations of life."

BELIEVE YOU ARE MORE THAN YOUR WEALTH

Living beneath your means is the only route to take
to enjoy a secure and comfortable standard of living
throughout your working and retirement years.
Living beneath your means isn't a suggestion.
It's an imperative.
— Jonathan D. Pond

I own very few things today.

Because I am more than the brand of my watch, the logo of my shoes, the name of my car. I believe that if in my soul I deeply respect and value myself, people around me will sense that, and they too will value and respect me — whether I'm wearing an Armani or not.

When I need a pair of jeans, I buy them from the market. No kidding. The last nameless pair I bought was P180. I admit it doesn't look as neat as a Levi's or a Diesel, but I don't think people will love me less than they do the guy whose jeans cost P2500.

I drive a "utility" vehicle that never gets stares from people because it's so ordinary. It has no power locks, power windows or power mirrors. I can park it

anywhere I want to. (No nagging worries for me.) I
don't get a heart attack if it gets scratched or bumped
because it's just a car: it brings me from point A to
point B.

I don't believe in luxury cars. I believe it's a crime
against oneself to buy a three-million-peso car — and
whether it's a crime to the poor is up to moral
theologians to argue about. All I'm saying is that
luxury cars just make your life complicated and
burdensome — and life is complicated enough as it is,
so why worsen it?

Before you buy anything, first think of the amount
of money, energy and time you'll need to maintain it,
dust it, insure it, clean it, protect it and fix it.

Believe me.

You are worth more than your wealth.

Action Plan

Do you feel a need to impress others by what you
wear?

Do you feel an attachment to material things?

Search for people you know who aren't attached to
material things but are happy, loving and free.
Interview them. Get some tips from them. Be inspired
by them. And pray for this grace.

DON'T BELIEVE YOUR DESIRES WHEN THEY SAY, "AFTER THIS, I'LL BE SATISFIED."

The wife said to the husband,
"This Christmas, let's give more practical gifts
to one another, like socks and a diamond ring."
—Anonymous

I love retelling my experience in Grade Four, when the inevitable "passage of manhood" happened in school: A few classmates of mine started wearing long pants. Suddenly, they looked so mature, so grown up, so *guwapo*[1] — while all of us who wore the uniform khaki shorts were so *totoy*.[2] So I pressed Mom to buy me a pair, but she kept on saying, "Later, Bo." The following year, I was in Grade Five, I was the *only* one wearing shorts. It was humiliating. In Grade Six, I was the only guy wearing a *bikini.* That's what my classmates called my shorts as I had already outgrown them.

---

[1] *handsome*
[2] *childish*

Believe me, I have never again been so sexy in my life.

Finally, on graduation day, I wept with pure joy when Mom gave me my very own pair of pants. Oh, I didn't care if the fold at the bottom of each leg was 12 inches long, even reaching up to my knees ("So that I can adjust them as you get taller," my mother explained.) To me, they were the most beautiful pair of long pants in the world.

But ironically, after a while, the thrill faded away. Because I started wanting to wear jeans.

"Mom, everyone has at least one pair!" I pleaded.

When she bought me one after a few years of begging, I soared to cloud nine and romped off in them like a prince. I thought my happiness would never end, until my high school classmates told me that their jeans were *Levi's* while mine were *Ludy's.*

But to this day, wearing Ludy's has been my happy lifestyle.

In fact, people ask me, "Why do you have so few desires in your life now?" The answer comes from my bikini experience: I've realized that all human desire never quits on you. We just keep on wanting more and more stuff. Nothing ever satisfies.

Never believe your desires when they say, "After this, I'll be satisfied."

Action Plan

What material things do you desire right now? Do you think you'd be satisfied once you've acquired them?

Try being satisfied without them now — because the truth is, if you're not satisfied without them now, you'll never be satisfied with them. Material things will never make you happy.

NEVER BUY ON CREDIT

Those who borrow are slaves of moneylenders.
— Proverbs 22:7

I don't believe in using credit cards. (For convenience, I use one card, but I pay the whole amount at the end of each month.) If I need something really bad, I save up for it. Sometimes, at midpoint, I realize I don't really need the darn thing and give up the whole idea. The only exception I feel we can enter into credit is in business and when buying a non-depreciating item, such as housing or land.

I believe we should always live below our earning capacity. Sure, that five-year-old car needs to visit the shop more often. But if you buy a new car, you'll be forking out 12 thousand pesos a month—for the next five years. I'd rather drive an old car, sleep comfortably at night, and invest my 12 thousand a month on time deposit, earning a minimum 6% compounded interest daily.

Get real: Don't be fooled by offers of "24 Easy Payments." There is no such thing as an "easy" payment. Believe me, every payment will be hard! So instead of *them* charging you interest, put your money in investments where *you* charge them interest!

Never buy on credit.

Action Plan

Do you have something you want to buy right now and are tempted to buy on credit? Don't! Save up for it every month. Tame your I-Want-It-Now monster. See what happens to your desire after a few months of saving.

GET TO ZERO-DEBT—FAST!

Many people have finally realized that money can't buy happiness. Now they're trying credit cards.
— Anonymous

In a while, I'm going to teach you how to save money by decreasing your expenses. But before you start a savings account, pay off all your debts as soon as you can with the money that you save. Why? Because you are paying more interest on your loans than earning interest from your savings! As of this writing, savings accounts give only an average of 3% monthly interest. Even if time deposits can push it to 8%, your housing loans can climb up to18% and credit card loans can go up to 24% a year and more! So put your savings into paying your debts!

List down all your debts from those with the highest interests down to the lowest ones. If you are paying off credit card loans, shop for credit cards that charge lower interests and transfer your loans there. I repeat: I don't like credit cards. But I'm giving you this tip as a process of paying off your debts, not as a permanent way of life.

Even as you are trying to pay off your higher -
interest loans as much as you can afford, try to pay the
lower-interest ones with the minimum amount. By
giving your creditors even a few hundred pesos a
month, you're telling them that you're not running
away. In fact, call them up and tell them you're
working on your finances.

I'll say it again: Save as much as you can from
your current expenses and pour it all in your debts.

Get to zero-debt — *fast*!

Action Plan

Do you dream of ever reaching the state of zero-
debt? Fire up this dream! Make a payment scheme
plan and calculate when you will reach zero-debt.
Print this date—month and year—in big, bold letters in
your journal. Have faith and stick to your plan.

GET HELP IF YOU'RE A CREDIT ADDICT

I owe, I owe, so off to work I go.
—Anonymous

Mary Hunt tells of her agonizing life as a credit-addict in her book *The Financially Confident Woman.* She was unemployed and $100,000 deep in debt when she made a choice to either give up using her credit cards or face financial ruin. Through determination and God's grace, she was able to rise from this trial and is now a financially confident woman!

Here's a checklist from her of what I call a credit-addict. See if any of these descriptions apply to you.

❏ I am always near the limit of my credit cards.
❏ I often use this month's income to cover last month's bills.
❏ I can't imagine living without credit.
❏ I worry about money quite a lot.
❏ I don't have a formal savings program.
❏ I have lied to my spouse or creditors about making payments.

❑ I know I should give money to God but there's
    just not enough right now.
❑ I've taken a cash advance on one credit card to
    make the payment on another card.

If you checked some or all of these items, get help,
quick! Ask friends to discipline you, help you tear up
your credit cards, and support you in your decision to
stay "sober" from borrowing money.

Get help if you are a credit addict.

Action Plan

If you are a credit addict, tear up your credit cards.
Call up friends you can be accountable to now. Read
Debt-Free Living by Larry Burkett.

Do you know of people who are credit addicts?
Pray for them.

GIVE AS MUCH AS YOU CAN

*My experience was that the less I spent on myself
and the more I gave to others,
the fuller of happiness and blessing did my soul become.*
— Hudson Taylor

Many years ago, I read this bumper sticker: *Live simply so that others may simply live.* The reasoning makes sense. If I content myself with a P250-shirt instead of a P3500 Lacoste, I can help others with my P3250. Trust me, there's immense pleasure! You'll find that the empty thrill of owning a diamond ring on your finger pales in comparison to the joy of handing a piece of bread to an orphan child.

And God is able to make all grace abound to you, so that in all things at all times, having all that you need, you will abound in every good work.

—2 Corinthians 9:8

Listen to me. I can't explain how it works *logically*, because giving and receiving a hundredfold blessing is a supernatural activity. In my experience, the more I give, the more I receive. It just works that way!

However, I don't give to receive. That's important.

I give because I believe it's right to give. As another bumper sticker declares, *"Tithe if you love Jesus. Any idiot can honk!"*

The Old Testament law of tithing, or giving 10% of your income, is a good guideline to follow. The New Testament challenges us to give with a cheerful heart. When you're cheerful, you may give more than 10%!

Make it a habit.

Give as much as you can.

Action Plan

Do you tithe?

If you think you're budget won't allow it, try a small token. Give it regularly. And then make it grow as you start living simply.

SAVE AS MUCH AS YOU CAN

If the goal is to give 10% to God, and it is,
why not dignify yourself with an equal portion?
Ten percent is yours to keep.
—Mary Hunt

I recommend that you save *at least* 10% of your income. I can almost hear you now: "Bo, that's impossible!" Oh yeah? Well, how did you live three years back, when your salary was smaller?

Sacrifice. Many of our needs are actually wants. Is cable TV a need? Will you suddenly die if you don't watch CNN or HBO? Are those new golf clubs essential to your existence? Will a larger-screen TV make you a better person?

Saving tames your I-want-to-have-it-now monster. It settles your spirit and makes you more confident about yourself and your future.

Invest in time deposits, long-term stocks and housing. Let me make the equation simple for you: If you save P2,000 a month for the next 20 years at 6% compounded monthly interest, you'll have around P1.5 million. Okay, so you want to object: "But what will 1.5 million pesos buy me 20 years from now? A tee-shirt?" Go ahead. Laugh. But 20 years from now, I'd rather walk around with 1.5 million pesos in my pocket than nothing.

Do yourself a favor.

Save as much as you can.

Action Plan

Do you have a formal savings program?

Make a decision now to set aside 10% of your monthly income, let it accumulate and never touch it except for real emergencies.

MAKE YOUR MONEY WORK FOR YOU

The magic of compounding interest
is truly the eighth wonder of the world!
— Albert Einstein

I'm going to give you an illustration. Supposing you're 21 years old, fresh from college, and your first job pays you a net salary of P6,000 a month.

Because you know the value of saving, you decide to take advantage of your situation. Since you're still living with your parents and don't have many "overhead" expenses, you decide to say "no" to materialistic pursuits and decide to be *ruthless*: you'll save P500 a month—and live on P5,500 for the basics of food, transportation, etc. It's going to be hard, but the goal in your mind keeps you going: You're saving for the future.

If you save P500 monthly at 6% annual interest compounded monthly and net of taxes, you'll have P290,234 at the end of 25 years. Fair enough?

Just to prove to you how magical the passage of time is towards your savings, even if you stopped saving at the age of 45 (let's say you decide to retire early so that you can serve the poor in India), your savings will continue to grow even without you putting any money in! Check out the table below.

What can I say? Saving works. The earlier you save, the better!

Age	Monthly Savings	Total Savings
20 yrs old	0 per month	P 0.00
21-25 yrs old	P500 per month	P 33,965.00
26-30 yrs old	P500 per month	P 77,123.00
31-35 yrs old	P500 per month	P 131,996.00
36-40 yrs old	P500 per month	P 201,685.00
41-45 yrs old	P500 per month	P 290,234.00
46-50 yrs old	0 per month	P 368,784.00
51-55 yrs old	0 per month	P 468,599.00
56-60 yrs old	0 per month	P 595,421.00
61-65 yrs old	0 per month	P 756,567.00
66-70 yrs old	0 per month	P 961,324.00
71 years old	0 per month	P1,221,498.00

Don't let others charge you interest.
Do that for them.

Make your money work for you.

Action Plan

Are you the impulsive type who withdraws from his savings account to buy a new DVD or a cool shirt from the mall? Look for a bank that is geographically far from your office or home, and don't apply for an ATM card, so that withdrawing will be inconvenient.

BE CREATIVE SAVERS

You lazy people can learn by watching an anthill.
—Proverbs 6:6

Here are a few great ways to save up for your future and become good stewards of your resources.

Automatic Savings

If you can arrange this with your employer and/or your local bank, you can ask them to regularly set aside a certain amount of your monthly salary for your savings—before you ever see it!

Save Your Raise

If your company gives you a raise, allot that additional amount to your savings account and live within your old paycheck. You'll see the fruits of this, even just after a year!

Keep Paying Loans After the Loans Are Paid Off

You've finished paying off the amortization of your car? Or that housing loan? Or that credit card loan? (You didn't read this book before making that loan, I'm sure.) Good. Keep sending the same amount, not to the creditors but to your savings account!

Hold On to Unexpected Cash

Received a bonus? An overdue reimbursement from the office? A cash gift from Mom and Dad? Keep this in your savings account—not in your wallet—because all wallets have invisible holes and money kept in them has been known to vanish within 24 hours.

Give up Expensive Habits

Imagine what you will save in one year if you give up smoking, buying Lotto tickets, eating an extra sweet snack (that's not helping your health anyway).

Sell Assets

You'll be freer if you sell all the clutter in your home—stuff that you no longer use! Liquidate. Get rid of that stuff.

Be inventive savers.

Action Plan

Which of the above suggestions can you practice? Any other creative ideas?

INVEST WISELY

Take all your savings and buy some good stock and hold it
until it goes up, then sell it. If it doesn't go up, don't buy it.
— *Will Rogers*

I'm no investment counselor. So whatever I say here is merely an encouragement for you to seek one out. (Don't get Will Rogers.) But after digesting a slew of financial and business books on the topic, I'm distilling the most basic principles in two rules:

First, never get into something you don't understand. Is there a friend inviting you into a business you know nothing about? Think twice and thrice and four times before jumping in. I'm saying this because I've seen many that have lost their whole life savings and retirement fund because they got into things they didn't understand.

Second, never put your life savings into high-risk investments. If you have negligible funds that you're prepared to lose, then go ahead—invest in that credit firm that offers a high 18% per annum. If you earn, good for you. If the firm crashes or the business folds up, you were ready for it. Be thankful it wasn't your life savings you put into it.

Invest wisely.

Action Plan

Are you losing sleep because a big part of your life savings is placed in high-risk investments? Get out of them as soon as you can. Your peace of mind is more valuable than all the money in the world.

DON'T TRY TO APPEAR WEALTHY

One day I had a sudden realization:
If I stopped buying things right this moment,
There is no way I could use all I have now.
— Don Aslett

In the best-selling book *Millionaires Next Door,* authors Thomas Stanely and William Danko were surprised to discover that real millionaires in the U.S. have very simple tastes. Let me say that again, lest you think that was a typo error: Most *real* millionaires have a simple lifestyle.

In their book, the *real* millionaire was not defined by how much money he earned — but by his net worth. (That is, by the wealth he could still call his own — through property, through investments, through savings, etc.) *Because you could earn buckets of cash but that doesn't mean you're wealthy.* You could earn millions but then still be buried in debt, still have financial worries and have a net worth of a doughnut — because you've been spending it all on deteriorating stuff.

Don't be shocked, but these authors found out that most of the *real* wealthy rarely wore designer clothes, rarely lived in expensive homes, rarely had expensive vacations and rarely bought luxury cars. So where did they put their money? They lived way below their earning capacity, so that they could save more and multiply their money through investments and business. Many of them saved 20% or more of their income! That meant simplifying their lives. Check this out:

According to their surveys, 66% of the buyers of foreign luxury cars were NOT truly wealthy. (Next time you see a *BMW* or a *Volvo* driving down the road, there's a good probability that the owner is living beyond his means and is paying through his nose in debt, with steep interest—and consequently, not enjoying a good night's sleep.) Most of the truly wealthy kept their ordinary cars for a number of years, and even 36% of them bought only second-hand cars!

Most of the really wealthy didn't reside in upscale villages. (One reason they gave was that residing in plush villages would pressure them to maintain an upscale lifestyle—something they didn't want to do.) And most didn't change homes for 30 years or more.

One of the most startling facts the authors found out: Most of the real wealthy stayed married to one spouse (no divorce, no alimony), and had a good family life. They trained their kids in the values of simplicity, frugality, and hard work.

Don't try to appear wealthy.

Action Plan

Are you comparing yourself with your richer neighbors and friends? Give up that nasty habit. Be happy with where you are and who you are.

52

BUDGET, BUDGET, BUDGET

> *A budget is a theological document.*
> *It tells you who or what you worship.*
> *— Anonymous*

If you aim for nothing, you'll get there.

And if you don't plan how you'll spend your money, you'll also end up in the same place financially: you'll have nothing at the end of the day.

First of all, track your spending. Before leaving for work, tuck into your pocket a little notebook where you can jot down expenses every time you purchase something. Each new day should have its own page. Tedious? Don't worry—you'll get the hang of it after a while; it'll be like second nature.

You're doing this because you want to *know* where your money goes. This "diagnosis" will give you the wisdom where to cut back and do some "surgery."

At the end of each month, pull out your tiny notebook and make a spreadsheet. (You can also use your computer for this.) Create categories: Food, House maintenance, Medical, Clothing, Tuition, etc.

Pencil down your expenses and voila, what you've got is a "spending record."

If you do this for about two or three months, you can now create a "spending plan" or budget—based on your diagnosis.

One guy who made a spending record for the first time was shocked to realize he could save P1,500 each month if he gave up his after-office-hours snack before returning home. "I deserve this because I work so hard," he reasoned—until he summed up the *yearly* savings if he went straight home to his wife and let her feed him from their kitchen.

This page won't be enough to teach you all that you need to learn about home budgeting. My suggestion is that you get a friend whose financial life is in order and ask her to help you develop your system.

And stick to your budget! Remember: The moment you get your salary, give your tithes first. Second, give to your savings account. Third, give to your "irregular expenses" account (see next page). If you don't make these your first bills, trust me, you won't be able to tithe or save at all.

Budget, budget, budget.

Action Plan

Do you have a budget?

Who can help you develop a budget? Call up that person now and set up an appointment.

CREATE AN "IRREGULAR EXPENSES" ACCOUNT

Worry is the interest we pay on tomorrow's troubles.
—E. Stanley Jones

There are expenses that don't come each month. Tuition fees lunge at you like a predator from the sky. Car insurance strikes when you thought you had your finances under control. Washing machine repairs attack you in the dead of night.

Solution?

Part of your budgeting is figuring out *what* these irregular expenses are in your life and knowing *how much* they cost in total each year. Divide this figure by 12 and that's what you should set aside in another account called "Irregular Expenses." Note: This isn't your savings account!

Okay, I know you want to strangle me for not telling you this sooner, but I had to give the bitter medicine to you slowly.

Yes, that means cutting back on your expenses some more.

Again, that means a change of attitude before you can change how you spend your money. But having an "irregular expense" account gives you the confidence and peace that you need to cope with every day.

Create an "Irregular Expenses" account.

Action Plan

Get your calculator now and start computing how much you need to set aside for your "irregular expenses" account.

BALANCE

Let all things be done decently and in order.
— 1 Corinthians 14:40

Balance. Don't take living simply to the extremes!
Living simply doesn't mean living in deprivation. It
doesn't mean eating from a can of sardines past its
expiry date, cutting off the electricity at home and
making do with candles and charcoal, and sewing
your ten-year-old curtains for your daughter's senior
prom dress.

Balance is so important that Janet Luhrs preaches
it in every single chapter of her huge 444-page book,
The Simple Living Guide!

There are special days when my wife and I eat in a
fancy restaurant. Or when we splurge on a vacation.
Very rare, yes, but my point is that you take living
simply NOT as a rigid goal—but as a happy process
towards the goals of generosity, inner peace and
holiness.

It really depends on your priorities.

As a couple, we've prioritized our health, so we
buy a lot of fruits and vegetables and health food that
tend to be pricier than the ordinary fare. So even if our

grocery bill is higher than we intended it to be, that's a choice we've deliberately made.

Consequently, we've cut back on the other items that don't appear in our top values — like clothes, accessories, appliances and gizmos.

That's the central point of living simply: we live deliberately.

Balance.

Action Plan

Is simplicity such an extreme thing for you that you're no longer loving people—especially those closest to you? Remember that simplicity isn't the goal—but peace of mind and love of neighbor. Review your lifestyle and make it more balanced.

DON'T WORK ONLY FOR THE MONEY

Normal is getting dressed in clothes that you buy for work,
driving through traffic in a car that you are still paying for,
in order to get to the job that you need so you can pay for the
clothes, car and the house that you leave empty all day in order
to afford to live in it.
— Ellen Goodman, Columnist

Many people are already working on something they love to do. But because they have a high-spending lifestyle, they have to shift careers in order to earn more. But the second career isn't what they love doing—so they end up richer but miserable.

But when we spend less, we can work less.

When we work less, we can play more.

When we play more, we can take the time to be better human beings.

We will earn money, but not at the expense of our faith, our loved ones and ourselves. The principle: **Satisfaction is not getting what you want, but wanting what you already have.**

A friend of mine is a salesman who has refused a managerial position for over 20 years now. He tells me that though he'd love the higher pay of a manager, he just doesn't see himself overseeing a lot of sales people. He explains that it isn't his gift. He wants to stick to what he does best: selling.

He keeps his needs simple and is satisfied with his job.

He is a very happy man.

Don't work only for the money.

Action Plan

Are you happy with your job?

What do you love to do? What is your passion?

Can you turn your passion into something that pays you?

DREAM YOUR LIFE-DREAMS

Most of the things worth doing in the world
had been declared impossible before they were done.
— Louis Brandeis

Simplicity means singularity of purpose. You're not scattering your energies all over the place doing unconnected and uncoordinated things.

A few years back, I decided to write a personal vision for my life. I went away for a while and prayed and wrote a picture of what kind of life I wanted to live 20 years down the road. I wrote about the kind of work schedule I'd keep, the relationships I'd nurture, the projects I'd want to create, the poor I'd want to help, the simple house I'd live in, the simple car I'd be driving, even the kind of person I'd like to become. I basically wrote down my life-dreams. And the little document that is kept in my computer is entitled as such: *Bo's Life-Dreams*.

I also believe I co-authored it with my Creator. I have a firm conviction that He is involved in my daily affairs, and He has dreams for my life.

I also summarized my mission in one statement: *to share a full life with others, especially with those who have it least, through preaching, writing, pioneering, friendship and family.* Every time I say it, I feel electricity come up my spine! I now stick to this mission. I don't manage companies, I don't do administration, I don't build buildings. I focus on my life purpose.

How do you discover your life-dreams?

First of all, discern the *holy desires* in your soul. Because deep down, you will desire the very things that you are supposed to be working on as your life-project. It may not be evident at first and it may take years for you to stumble upon it, but once the vision takes hold of you, you cannot but move towards that direction. Your mission will fit you perfectly.

Second, discern the *raw materials* that you are gifted with. When you are appointed to a sacred task, you will find an anointing in that area that blesses many people. Suddenly, you realize that all your training, all your trials, all your experiences were a preparation for this life-project that was waiting for you all along.

Third, discern the *open doors of circumstances.* There will be opportunities that will open up before you to take your first steps towards the fulfillment of your life-dreams. Be open. Persevere. And have faith.

What kind of life do you really want?

Do you want to travel?

Meet new people and share life and love?

Operate a retreat house by the seaside?

Adopt and live with 12 orphans in a huge house?

Write a novel that will inspire thousands?

Work part-time so that you have more opportunities for helping the poor?

Start a small catering service?

Build your own cottage on an island?

Set up your own school?

Be a full-time mother to your children—and your children's friends?

Go on and dream your life-dreams.

Action Plan

Do you know what your life-dreams are?

Schedule a few hours for this endeavor; a weekend retreat is even better! (Use the instructions and questions in this chapter and in the next one as a guide for this personal retreat.) Get your date book and cross out that day with a fat red pen. No one touches that day. It's your date where you discuss your life with God.

DISCOVER YOUR LIFE-DREAMS

Whether you turn to the right or to the left,
your ears will hear a voice behind you,
saying, "This is the way; walk in it."
— Isaiah 30:21

Take an extended time of personal reflection and bring these questions with you.

It's important that you write your answers.

- What are your greatest strengths?

- What is that primary gift that has been given to you so you can bless the world?

- What do you enjoy doing the most?

- What were the happiest moments of your life? What were you doing during those moments?

- If given an opportunity to live in any way and do anything—no matter how crazy your choice would be—what kind of life would you choose to live?

Imagine yourself on your 75th birthday.
- What kind of person would you want to be by that time?

- What accomplishments would you want to have attained?

- If family members were to honor you on your 75th birthday party and thank you and speak about the good things that you have done, *what would you want them to say to you?*

From your answers above, write a tentative personal mission statement. This one sentence should express what you most deeply believe you should attain at the end of your days. *It should be inspiring and moving as well.* And don't worry if it won't be perfect. Your personal mission statement should undergo much revision and editing as the weeks, months and years go by. You should review your personal mission statement in prayer regularly.

Finally, write down your life-dreams.

Now that you've written down a personal mission statement, write down a description of your life five, ten, 20 years down the road. Picture yourself, your schedule, your work, your house, your relationships, your projects, your character in vivid detail. Don't worry if you fill a few pages for your life-dreams. Let your heart speak as you paint on the canvas of your imagination.

Discover your life-dreams.

Action Plan

Answer the questions above in your little retreat. Bring your journal with you and write your answers there.

If you already know your life-dreams, reflect on them again. See if your daily life follows them and receives from them power and direction. Perhaps you need to rediscover your life-dreams if you've forgotten them through the years.

CREATE YOUR FINANCIAL PLAN BASED ON YOUR LIFE-DREAMS

Begin with the end in mind.
—Stephen Covey

After writing my life-dreams document, I then wrote my financial plan: How much I should be earning by this year, how much I should be earning by next year, how much I should be earning by the third year and so on. Because I knew what I wanted to do with my life, I also had an idea how much money it would take to support my life-purpose.

Writing down a financial goal is an exercise in faith. And an exercise in personal commitment. My mind was forced to open up and think of ways how those goals would be met. Believe me, it was as though power was being released as I wrote my financial goals. But as I scribbled on paper every crazy idea that came to my mind, I repeatedly kept going back to my divinely appointed mission in life—

because that was how God was going to provide for me.

Let me explain.

I believe that when we're faithful to our mission and give ourselves to the world and genuinely help people live a better life, we see the world repay us. When we give, we receive — and we just don't receive, we receive much more than what we have given. This law of reciprocity is written in the fabric of the universe.

Naturally, for this law of reciprocity to work, you need to *charge what you are worth* and not undersell yourself. If you are working in business, I believe that you should get the highest pay you can get for your work. Earning money doesn't make you less spiritual. If the money that you're going to earn is to support your God-appointed life-dreams, it *is* very spiritual. (It's another issue altogether to be working for a religious ministry or a philanthropic organization where you are *voluntarily* underselling yourself, choosing rather to pick up non-monetary rewards in the after life.)

So far, I've been able to attain my financial goals — enough to support my family and more than enough to be generous to those in need — this second item being an intrinsic part of my mission.

But more importantly, by creating a financial plan based on my life-dreams, I live *deliberately*, and money is still connected to my mission—not something apart from it. Because success for me isn't having the greatest wealth but the fulfillment of my life-dreams—90 percent of which *aren't* financial.

Create your Financial Plan based on your life-dreams.

Action Plan

Do you know how much money you will need next year? Two years from now? If you've finished writing your life-dreams, set aside time to write your financial goals based on this vision statement. Pray to God to help you in this task, inspiring you toward different ways you can attain them.

DO WHAT YOU LOVE AND GET PAID FOR IT

There can be no joy of life without joy of work.
— St. Thomas Aquinas

We give 60% of our waking time to our jobs. If we're unhappy with our jobs, that makes us unhappy 60% of our lives!

To simplify our lives, we need to find what we love doing and get paid for it.

We need to find out what our passion is and connect it with our jobs.

As a writer, my research demands that I read hundreds of books a year. But that's fine by me because I love reading. Even if my job was something else, I'd still read a horrendous lot because I enjoy it immensely. Don't laugh, but my favorite fantasy is being a security guard assigned to protect an isolated island — where there is nothing else to do but read books all day.

I remember calling up our finance director at ten o'clock in the evening. I asked him, "Am I disturbing you?" and he answered, "No problem. I'm just relaxing."

"Watching TV?" I inquired.

"Nope, just balancing the accounting books of our organization."

I almost fell from my chair. "That's your way of relaxing?"

He said it was. He feels most alive and happy holding a pencil, a calculator, and reams of paper filled with numbers and nothing else. This was his passion, and it was his privilege that this was his job as well. He'd do it even if he weren't paid for it. (I told him that we're opposites in this regard. If I'm left with nothing else to look at but numbers for even just an hour, I'd suffer a nervous breakdown.)

I am doing work which is worth doing. It would still be worth doing if nobody paid for it. But as I have no private means, and need to be fed and housed and clothed, I must be paid while I do it.

— C.S. Lewis,
Good Work and Good Works

But making your passion your job isn't only enjoyable. It may be your best bet to provide adequately for your needs and earn extra for generosity.

According to one study of millionaires, an impressive majority eventually became wealthy not because they

possessed a primary ambition to get rich, but because they found work about which they could be passionate. Their "luck" arose from their dedication to an area they enjoyed. The universe bends to those who are convinced that they are in the right place doing the right thing...
— Allan Loy Mcginnis,
The Balanced Life

Do what you love and get paid for it.

Action Plan

What is your passion? What is the one thing that you love to do, where you feel most alive?

Can you turn this passion into your profession? Can you visualize it? If yes, write down the steps that you need to take to make this dream come true.

CONNECT YOUR JOB TO YOUR LIFE-MISSION

"Then the Lord your God will make you
most prosperous in all the work of your hands."
– Deuteronomy 30:9

A friend of mine was working with technical and building maintenance. He spent most of his working hours with his screwdrivers, soldering irons and hammers. But after five o'clock, before proceeding home, he'd visit his "pals" in the seedy parts of the city. Whenever he saw a group of street kids, he bought a loaf of bread, sat down with them in the sidewalk and talked about life.

He had a passion to help street kids, a passion to see them become better human beings. It didn't take him long to realize this was his mission in life. Could he make it his job as well?

The answer was yes. Soon after this, he resigned from his job. Today, together with his wife, my friend feeds 70 street kids in his home every day. And with his talent for making stuff with his own hands, he helps the children learn new skills as well. He writes his own fundraising letters, gets support from generous individuals and helps the kids go to school. It is a tough life, and there are days when finances are low, but he doesn't regret his decision one bit.

I have another friend who is a nurse by profession but loves music so much he practically wakes up and sleeps with his keyboard synthesizer. He feels that his mission is to play music and fill the souls of men with God's melody. The solution? He works as a private nurse—not for a hospital—which gives him the freedom to work part-time as a musician for a religious organization and even take a few gigs in the entertainment business.

I believe that we are created for a mission, and that mission has been prepared for us beforehand. It is waiting for us to fulfill it!

For we are God's workmanship, created in Christ Jesus to do good works, which God prepared in advance for us to do.

—*Ephesians 2:10*

If we can connect our mission to our occupations, we may just be the happiest of people on this planet.

Action Plan

What is your mission in life? Discover the raw materials that you have been gifted with by life. How do these skills and talents contribute to a better world? Can they lift up the quality of life of people? Can you turn this into your job?

FIND YOUR "FLOW"

To be in the flow is to be unself-consciously absorbed.
Think of a situation where you get so caught up in an activity
that your mind doesn't wander, that you become oblivious to your
surroundings, and time flies.
—David Myers

What do these great achievers, e.g. Mozart, who had 600 compositions; Thomas Edison, who had 1,093 inventions; and Isaac Asimov, who wrote 475 books, have in common? They have found their "flow." What does *flow* mean? Look at the chart below.

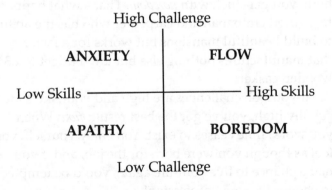

(From Mihaly Csikszentmihalyi and Isabella Selega Csikszentmihalyi, *Optimal Experience: Psychological Studies of Flow of Consciousness,* as quoted by David Myers, *The Pursuit of Happiness*)

If your job challenges are high but your skills are abysmally low, the result is *anxiety.* That's what happens to the new salesman who faints every time he faces a client. He should either get a new job that matches his skills — like as a mattress quality tester for some bed manufacturer — or get training to upgrade his skills in selling.

If your job challenges are low and your skills are low as well, you'd get *apathy.* An example would be an accountant who doesn't even know how to use a calculator but doesn't worry one bit about losing his job because his father owns the business.

If your job challenges are low but your skills are high, you get stuck with *boredom.* That's what happens to a gifted craftsman and carpenter who has the ability to build beautiful mansions but works for a factory that manufactures nothing else but low-budget 6"x 3" wooden caskets.

If your job challenges are high and your skills are equally high, you've got the best result: *flow.* When you work, time ceases to exist. You enjoy yourself, you feel as though you were born for the job, and if you had a chance to live your life again, you'd be tempted to choose the same profession!

Find your flow.

Action Plan

Evaluate your present job right now. Does it give you enough challenge? And do you have enough skills to match those challenges? If you see an inequality, what can you do about it?

MAKE SOME MONEY

All hard work brings a profit...
—Proverbs 14:23

You might wonder what this chapter has to do with simplifying your life.

You see, I receive tons of letters from readers, most of them happy, but some of them heart-rending. Just yesterday, one letter I read was from a man who was poor all his life. He didn't even know how he'd get food for his family the following week. Sure he had a job, but it paid miserably and wasn't even enough to keep his kids in school. I opened another letter the other day and read about a woman who had so many debts her monthly payables were double her monthly income. And according to her, she was already living very, very, very simply! She hasn't bought a new dress in ages, never went to movies unless it was a freebee, and had sold most of her belongings.

Not having enough money for your basic needs isn't the simple life. That's poverty, and that complicates life.

Read carefully. Money isn't everything and people are totally mistaken if they think that money will solve all their problems and make them happy. But we do *need* a minimum amount of money in order to live. It is because of letters like these that I wish to share with you now the six key principles of making money — without robbing your soul.

The next six chapters of this book will be devoted to the six steps on how you can make money. They are as follows:

1) Purify your thinking towards money
2) Purify your motives towards making money
3) Take on an abundance mentality
4) Believe in your capacity to make money
5) Make yourself more valuable
6) Discover something that you have that others need.

Simplify your life.
Make some money.

Action Plan

Are you living simply and yet still can't fit your income to your very simple expenses? It doesn't have to be this way. You don't have to accept this "complication" in your life forever. Write down in your journal, "I believe that I can raise my earning potential."

PURIFY YOUR THINKING TOWARDS MONEY

...we gave you this rule:
"If a man will not work, he shall not eat."
—2 Thessalonians 3:10

The first step to making money is to *purify your thinking towards money.*

If somewhere in your brain you think that money is evil, that it is unspiritual to earn money, then somehow, even subconsciously, you will find ways of avoiding money. I'm serious! But the Bible doesn't say that money is evil; the *love of money* is. Money is a neutral thing that can be used to love or hate, to build or destroy, depending on how you use it. In other words, it can make you holy or it can make you evil — much like anything else in life. It all depends on whether you follow or violate the laws written in the fabric of the universe concerning its use.

Purify your thinking towards money by embracing the truth that God *wants* you to have some material things to live a humane life, enough for your needs and more than what you need, so that you can be generous.

Make a faith statement that your Creator wants to provide for your needs.

Make a faith statement that God *wants* you to work and earn for a living and be responsible towards your family.

Also, it is important to watch your attitude towards those who are earning well. Do you resent them? Do you feel that they are unspiritual? Do you feel that they used deception to earn that kind of money? If you continue to have these thoughts, you're telling yourself that money indeed is bad and unspiritual and can only be made through deception.

Banish these thoughts.

Purify your thinking towards money.

Action Plan:

How do you view money? Do you associate it with good or bad, or both? Do you have a fear of money? Write your thoughts in your journal. Try to clarify now your biases by speaking the truth to yourself. Write down your faith statements.

PURIFY YOUR MOTIVES TOWARDS MAKING MONEY

We sow our thoughts,
and we reap our actions.
We sow our actions,
And we reap our habits.
We sow our habits,
and we reap our character.
We sow our character,
and we reap our destiny.
        —Anonymous

Motives need to come from our highest values if we want to live freely.

Ask yourself: **Why do you want more money**?

To provide for the basic needs of your family?

To fulfill your God-given responsibility as spouse and parent?

To be more generous to those in need?

To have more personal freedom to love?

When you inwardly feel that your motives are in line with your highest values, then you'll approach your moneymaking endeavors as a whole person. You will move and walk and talk with integrity. With peace and happiness! The journey will be pleasurable.

But if you inwardly feel that your motives are *not* in line with your highest values, then you will work towards earning money as a divided person. If your innermost motive for earning more money is merely for selfish opulence, your highest values will rebel against that and you'll experience a loss of integrity— a disintegration in your character. You may reach your financial goals, but you will never be at peace.

The solution?

Follow your conscience and change your motives according to your highest values.

Earn money with nobility.

Make money without robbing your soul.

Purify your motives towards making money.

Action Plan

Be honest. Examine your motives towards earning money and write them down in your journal. Silence yourself, read each motive you wrote down and pause to allow your conscience to speak.

TAKE ON AN ABUNDANCE MENTALITY

I will surely make you prosper and will make your descendants like the sand of the sea, which cannot be counted.
—Genesis 32:12

There's enough money out there!

Some people are trapped into a "scarcity" mentality; they think you have to be crafty, crooked, dishonest and underhanded to earn the little money that is floating around. That's not true. God has created an ample world, enough for everyone.

Make money by taking on an abundance mentality. All around you are opportunities to earn money. Vast opportunities! But in order to see them, you need to train your mind to think that there *are* opportunities out there. If you believe that there are none or that there are very few, then you'll have an incredibly hard time finding those moneymaking opportunities. *Because your mind will start looking for things that will prove your expectations and worldview!*

Change your expectations. Think abundance.

Just for fun, during one summer vacation, I enrolled our children from the orphanage for three-

week vocational courses at a government-run school.
The choices were many, but my little girls took up
cosmetology and one guy took up air-conditioning
maintenance. They still had their regular schooling
ahead of them, so they weren't studying these courses
to work but just to expand their horizons. But I was
amazed at the promise and hard work of this little
government school: After graduation, they'd actually
assist the students to find them real jobs. And my kids
had classmates who started working and earning
money on their own *before* they even graduated from
that measly three-week course!

But when we drove back home and passed
through the little barrio where our orphanage is
located, I saw the same sorry sight I see every day:
jobless people sitting in front of their bamboo shacks,
doing nothing. I remember asking some of them,
"Why don't you apply for work?" and they'd tell me,
"I didn't finish school." When I encouraged them to
study something—anything—they'd say they don't
have money, they don't have the time, they don't have
the courage…

But in reality, they're trapped in a scarcity
mentality. They believe the rich have cornered the
wealth of this world and they now can only collect the
breadcrumbs that fall from their table.

That's not true.

Money is everywhere.

Take on an abundance mentality.

P.S. This is *not* the prosperity gospel that I'm preaching. I don't adhere to the gospel that some preachers proclaim, wherein Jesus was super-wealthy and His disciples were super-wealthy and that every Christian should be super-wealthy. That's plain nonsense.

But I believe that God has provided *enough* for our needs and *more than enough* to be generous *if we open ourselves to that provision and work.*

Action Plan

Do you feel that there is money out there waiting for you? And do you believe that it's just a matter of hooking up yourself to the right opportunity?

Write a financial goal for yourself for the next year. No, don't just think about it—write it down! And then stretch your mind and plan how you can make that goal a reality. Remember that these plans must be in line with your highest values. It may take longer to reach your financial goals, but the fruit of following your integrity will far outweigh the monetary rewards.

BELIEVE IN YOUR CAPACITY TO MAKE MONEY

Wealth is the product of man's capacity to think.
—Ayn Rand

Remember that your *perception* of yourself is your *reality*. How you define yourself will be how you will act. If you believe that you're a lazy, inept, weak, dim-witted individual—that's how you will act. Your definitions of yourself are self-fulfilling prophecies. Why? Because as human beings, one of our greatest needs is consistency. You will find yourself acting *consistently* with your self-concept and self-definition.

The most vivid experience I had with this incredible truth came during my student years many years ago.

All my life, I defined myself as a C student. My most sublime goal in school was to get a grade past 75%. Why? Because that was my self-concept. I never saw myself as academic, studious or intelligent. That wasn't me.

But something happened along the way. On my third year in college, I had to quit for a while to work full time for a community project. One day, someone asked me if I wanted to take up post-graduate studies in theology as night classes. I told him I wasn't qualified because I wasn't a college graduate. But when the dean of the school talked to me and learned about my volunteer work, he said I could take the course if I wanted to. They'd just keep my Masters diploma until I finished my college degree.

But in those classes, I was surrounded by priests, nuns and seminarians, and my mind was challenged. My paradigm shift took place after my first exam. Our professor wrote down on the blackboard the five top students of the test. I wasn't even paying attention until someone tapped my shoulder to take a look. I found my name in the number one position, beside the words "perfect score." I couldn't believe my eyes.

After class, I remained glued to my seat, still gazing at that blackboard. My whole being was in shock. "You mean all this time," I reprimanded myself, "I was wrong? That I *can* be bright?"

That day changed my life. My self-concept was transformed forever. I went through that Masters program picking up A's every time I took an exam. I then went back to the last two years of my college years with a *vengeance.* Whatever class I took, be it statistics, science, philosophy or literature, I was in the honors list. I was a changed man!

Let me go back to the topic of this chapter: If in your thinking you *believe* that you can't earn enough money for your family, then you won't. If you see yourself as a C employee or worse, an F businessman, then that's what you will be. If this is your self-concept, then that'll be your life forever. Sometimes, people are trapped in a vicious cycle of poverty, handed down in their families from one generation to another. Their very *family identity* is indelibly wedged and welded with poverty. They see themselves, define themselves, describe themselves as poor. I've seen this phenomenon so many times in my work, I think it's an epidemic.

I am totally convinced that we are limited by our own core beliefs, and if we have small beliefs about ourselves, then we will remain small forever.

But if you believe in your heart that you can create money, then you can.

Your Creator has given you this capacity to earn money — for yourself, for your family, for your life-dreams. Use it!

Create a paradigm shift for yourself right now.

Believe in your capacity to make money.

Action Plan

Examine your self-concept. How do you define yourself? How do you describe yourself? Write down your answers.

MAKE YOURSELF
MORE VALUABLE

*The single most important and potent way to expand your income
is to devise a way to consistently add real value
to people's lives, and you will prosper.
— Anthony Robbins*

Believe that you have value.

Believe that you have something to give to the world.

All individuals who earn good money are persons who have found ways to add worth and value to their lives — and *then* make this worth and value *useful* to others. If you can add to your life more skills, more ability, more intelligence, more creativity, more caring and personalized service, more organized systems — and thereby increase the quality of life for the people around you — you'll be able to earn more money.

I'm not just talking about entrepreneurs. If you're employed right now, *make yourself more valuable to your company.* Don't expect a raise every year simply because you show up every workday! Develop your job skills, learn new ones, look for ways to improve your company's products and systems, search for procedures to make the work of your boss easier and think of ways where your company can save money.

I know of someone who entered as a clerk in one of the biggest companies in the country. This guy simply didn't stop making himself more valuable, he enrolled in any course he found useful to his profession. His bosses noticed his drive and kept giving him new responsibilities until he ended up as the company's assistant vice president. Sound like a fairy tale? Not to me. I'm talking about my father.

If you are self-employed, ask how your business can touch and bless the lives of your customers. Again, by making your business more valuable to people, earning profit can be the only consequence. My friend expanded his restaurant business considerably when he asked what his customers wanted to eat and at what prices. He asked questions. He took down notes. He experimented. Marketing people will say that he did a market analysis, but in my language, he simply learned how to love his customers in a better way.

Make yourself valuable.

Action Plan

If you are employed, how valuable are you to your company? How can you make yourself more valuable to your company?

If you are self-employed, how valuable are you to your customers? How can you make yourself more valuable to them?

DISCOVER SOMETHING THAT YOU HAVE THAT OTHERS NEED

Do you see a man skilled in his work?
He will serve before kings; he will not serve before obscure men.
—Proverbs 22:29

You have something that people need.

I don't know what *that* is, but I know it's there.

This is the basis of the entire world of business.

This is why people like you and me can make a living, work in jobs and earn a profit. *"Having something that people need"* is the foundation of any trade—whether it's the guy selling peanuts down the street or the multi-billion corporate empires of the world.

You have something that people need, and you need to discover what that something is. It could be some latent talent or skill or preference that you have. It could be your creativity. Or your patience. Or your dreams. Or your cooking. Or your talkativeness. Or your silence. Or your knowledge. Or your hobbies. Or your interests. Or your tastes.

And somewhere out there, someone needs what you have—and someone's willing to pay good money for what you have.

The simple life is not poverty. The simple life also means earning efficiently—utilizing the least amount of time and energy for the most profit—so that you have time for spiritual growth, enriching family life and loving service to brethren. I'm not talking about giving in to greed or overcharging. I'm talking against underselling yourself and being inefficient in your use of time.

I know of a friend who was an excellent religion teacher in a school. For years, he loved sharing his faith to his students. But one day, his youngest child acquired a severe illness that needed expensive medical care, something he couldn't afford with his current pay. Forced to look for a more profitable income, he asked himself what he had that others needed. One day, it just clicked in his brain: he's a great teacher, but this time, he can teach professionals.

Today, my friend is an in-demand speaker at human resource seminars, giving self-development courses for executives to rank and file employees all over the country. On the side, he impacts them with his faith perspective.

I know of someone else who wanted to give jobs to the poor people who lived around her home. She always loved artwork and so directed her attention in that field. With some encouragement from her husband, she designed some very simple gift items using native material and entered a big-time exhibit in Manila. In her mind, she doubted whether anyone would like her very plain and easy-to-make creations. But in that exhibit, an English businessman saw her products, liked them and made his first order.

Her little "hobby" is now a successful export business that gives livelihood to 80 poor families!

You see what I mean? Discover something that you have that others need.

Action Plan

What do you have that others observe as significant, beautiful, useful and very good? First, expand whatever *that thing* is. Increase it. Multiply it. Enhance it. And second, do some research. How do others who also have what you have make a living from it? Continue to be open.

BELIEVE IN YOUR PRODUCT

> *Demanding that people love us because we cannot*
> *love ourselves is an iron-clad guarantee of further rejection.*
> —Judith Viorst

If you won't believe in your product, no one else will.

One early dawn, I woke up terrified that I was going to address a crowd of ten thousand people. No, the size didn't bother me. By that time, I was used to it. What bothered me was that the organizers who invited me to speak wanted me to do so in pure *Tagalog*[1].

I'm ashamed to say this, but they could have asked me to speak in ancient Greek for all I cared, and it would have been almost the same. As a Filipino, I naturally speak conversational Tagalog, but because I didn't grow up in the Tagalog speaking regions of the country, I have never actually given a talk in pure Tagalog, to ten thousand people at that. I was petrified!

But as a public speaker, I also knew that it would be a disaster to go up the stage in the state of mind I

---

[1] *A Filipino language*

was in. If I stood in front of them doubting my ability, I'd never be able to impart my message. I'd also stutter, fumble with the microphone wire and drown in my own sweat. And my audience would fall asleep or talk about last night's ball game.

Because I knew the rule: If I don't believe in my product, no one else will.

So I closed my eyes and began to imagine myself giving that Tagalog talk with awesome fluency. I pictured in my mind the audience being inspired and moved by my stories. My visualizing worked so well, I was even *feeling* the inner elation of speaking well. I mentally told myself, "Gosh, you're a great Tagalog speaker, Bo."

I then prayed and believed that this would be my reality.

A few minutes later, I was on stage. And my vision did become reality!

I was more dynamic than usual. Ten thousand people were at the edge of their seats, listening to me. More importantly, I found myself fluent in Tagalog. Sure I made a lot of grammatical mistakes (only practice can cure that), but the important thing was that I wasn't distracted by them and neither were my listeners.

Why? Along the way, I've learned a secret about our minds I want to share with you. Our subconscious doesn't know the difference between what we experience and what we vividly imagine. As Richard Eyre would say in his book *Lifebalance*, "Our subconscious doesn't know the difference between something that *happens* and something that is *thought.*"

That's why Olympic champions use visualization exercises. Before the actual event, runners imagine themselves crossing the finish line. Swimmers *feel* what it would be like to be the first one to touch the swimming pool tiles at the end of their race. Weightlifters visualize themselves carrying the heaviest poundage ever.

They repeat these visualizations thousands of times.

So why can't we?

I believe that no matter what job we hold, we are in the business of selling something. As employees, we are selling our services to our companies. As entrepreneurs, we are selling goods we either manufactured or bought from another entrepreneur. But these things—our services and our goods—are but secondary products.

Our most important product is ourselves.

Close your eyes. Visualize that you are the masterpiece of this universe, fashioned by the Creator, in His beautiful image.

Believe in your product.

Action Plan

Do you believe in your product? In your capacity to serve and bless others?

Do a visualization exercise. Close your eyes and picture the best that you can be. What kind of person do you want to be? See that person in your mind. Feel what it means to be that person, *now.*

KEEP LOOKING FOR THE OPEN DOOR

> *No one can make you feel inferior*
> *without your consent.*
> —Eleonor Roosevelt

You won't close every sale, no matter what you do.

Some people won't like you.

In fact, along the way, you'll get lambasted, criticized, ridiculed.

In a word, you'll be rejected.

Well, I have another word for you: reject the rejection. Because somewhere near that door that just shut you'll find an open door. So keep on looking.

One day, a man was taking a train ride feeling dejected because he wasn't accepted at this writing job he was applying for. The editor who evaluated his work said he "lacked creativity." In that train ride, this man was doodling in his little note pad and a little mouse was born on that piece of paper. That mouse's name was Mickey, and that man's name was Walt Disney.

Do you think Albert Einstein was esteemed by all his teachers and classmates alike? Think again. As a kid, one professor said Albert's grades were very mediocre, he was the most likely student to amount to nothing.

Thomas Edison had more than a thousand failed experiments before he invented the light bulb. A thousand! It was he who said, "Our greatest weakness lies in giving up. The most certain way to succeed is always to try just one more time." He reaped the fruit of that principle as he has, aside from that light bulb, 1,092 inventions under his name.

I've failed more times than Edison. In the past 20 years, as a leader of five organizations, I've made many mistakes, and some people hated me for them. (I've also made a lot of good decisions and some people hated me for them as well!) At any one point in my life, I simply could have given in to my fears and threw in the towel and said, "That's it. I'm quitting." But I don't have to follow my fears if the deepest voice in my heart says, "Go on. Do what's right."

In any job, whether it be sales or accountancy, rejection is a given. It's merely a question of when it will come, from whom and how you're going to respond to it.

The best response is to keep on looking for the open door.

If you've got something that people need and you advertise it, people will be opening their doors to you.

You don't have to close every sale to succeed.

Keep on looking for the open door.

Action Plan

Have you experienced some rejection? They've lost a wonderful opportunity to work with you and gain your services. Keep walking. Keep searching. There's a lucky person out there, a fortunate company out there who will receive your blessing. Write down now a long list of other doors you can look into.

EMBRACE YOUR FEAR, BUT DO IT ANYWAY

> *The truth of the matter is that you always know*
> *the right thing to do. The hard part is doing it.*
> —*General H. Norman Schwarzkopf*

I don't know what your fears are, but I know mine. I fear people. I never realized how afraid I am of people. Especially angry people. I hate conflict. So I try to please everybody, which of course is a failed project from the very start.

But I've learned the hard way that I need to allow myself to feel that fear every time it comes, and befriend it. Yes, I feel my fear all the way. Every drop of it. I don't shoo it away, I don't escape, I don't forget about it, I don't drown it with ice cream and a TV sitcom.

I embrace my fear.

Why? I believe that feelings are symptoms that need to be heard. They carry an important message if we listen to them. Feelings that don't get heard fuel addictions—whether it is to drugs, alcohol, sex, eating (or not eating), shopping and materialism… You name it and it can be an escape from feeling our unpleasant emotions.

My fears have been teaching me about my childhood traumas, and I've begun to accept and love myself. Accepting my brokenness has made me a healthier human being.

But guess what I do *after* I feel my fears.

I do the right thing anyway.

My emotions are my best friends, not my cruel masters.

In my decision making, I still follow my highest values—not my noisiest emotions.

As a leader, I have made tough choices. Some of these choices were unpopular: reprimanding an employee, reorganizing a department, writing on a very sensitive topic that may offend some people...

Thinking about the potential anger, the conflicts, and the negative outcome stirs up fear like volcanic lava gurgling in my gut. It is overwhelming. Everything within me is screaming: Don't do it! You'll create conflict! People will not like you!

But I do it anyway.

And every time, I thank God I did.

Embrace your fears but do it anyway.

Action Plan

What are your fears? Have they prevented you from doing what you've always believed you should do?

Have you been running away from these fears? Escaping from feeling them through denial or avoidance, or worse, through addictions?

Make a choice now to face these fears. And make a choice to "do it anyway."

WATCH OUT FOR SIGNS OF BURNOUT

The mass of men lead lives of quiet desperation.
— Henry David Thoreau

Burnout is expensive. I know from personal experience. It cost me my health, my relationships, the vibrancy of my faith and happiness of work.

Burnout is such a common problem today that I'm devoting four chapters to this topic to explain how you should...

1) watch out for symptoms of burnout,
2) watch out for the causes of burnout,
3) deal with the two sides of burnout,
4) and burn up, not burn out!

Today, I stay clear of burnout by watching for the signs that I had during that difficult season of my life. See if you have any of them:

- I was always tired. Even after waking up in the morning, after a supposedly good night's rest, I woke up already exhausted and drained.
- I dreaded going to the office.
- I became depressed. Many times, I felt helpless at the difficulties and conflicts that I was facing at work.

- I doubted myself so much. I lost confidence and wondered what in the world I was doing in my job. I wanted out.
- I was more susceptible to psychosomatic illnesses, like frequent colds, stomach problems, etc.

Researchers state that there are certain professions that are prone to burnout, such as high-pressure business positions, as well as the helping professions: doctors, nurses, clergy, missionaries, counselors, social workers and teachers.

When you see these symptoms and if you are in any one of these professions, you know that you're a prime candidate for burnout. If so, you need to apply the lessons in this book *immediately.*

Watch out for the signs of burnout.

Action Plan

Do you see any of the symptoms indicated above in your life right now? Start slowing down. Decide to radically change certain attitudes and behaviors that are leading you to this dangerous path.

Do you see any of these symptoms among your family and friends? Gently share your concern with them.

WATCH OUT FOR THE CAUSES OF BURNOUT

*If you can't get your work done in 24 hours,
work nights!*
—lapel button

Let me share with you now the causes of my burnout. Find out if any of them look familiar to you. Remember that this is simply *my* experience and therefore other factors may trigger another person's burnout. But sharing these circumstances with you will give you an idea and spur you on to explore your own life for possible causes.

As I reflected on my ordeal, there were *internal* and *external* causes—and this is important to know because healing your burnout by changing your environment won't solve your problems if your burnout has internal causes. You could change jobs and even go to another country and still experience burnout in your next job and company if you don't deal with the inner attitudes that need changing.

Internal Causes:

- I had low self-worth. I used my achievements to cover up my need for affirmation and love from others, but no matter how much success I had at work, my broken self-image kept asking for more.

- I had ambition, driven by my low self-worth. I had so much drive, I could work for 16 hours straight.

- I had an overwhelming fear of conflicts and rejection, and so avoided problems and conflicts. I needed love so much, I didn't want anyone to get angry at me—so I tried my very best and exhausted every means to please everyone. Naturally, that goal was impossible and will always be impossible.

External Causes:

- I had a weak or vacillating leadership in the office. In my case, that was me! I was the boss, and I managed the office in a wishy-washy way. But working for a boss like me causes burnout as well. And according to psychologists, working for the other extreme— an authoritarian and demanding boss—can also produce burnout.

- I had chronic conflicts with co-workers. Conflicts are normal in our world, but when they become prolonged and unresolved, they can cause burnout.
- Low morale in the office was pervasive.
- There was poor communication between the different parts of my organization.

If you are familiar with these causes, you have more chances of avoiding burnout.

Watch out for the causes of burnout.

Action Plan

Do you see any of these factors or similar ones in your work and life? List them down in your journal and write down your feelings about each of them.

126

- Place choice together with co-workers conflict in the formal group would call when they become powerful and overwhelmed they become burnout.
- How morale in the place was perceived.
- There was poor communication between certain stakeholders of my organization.

If you are familiar with these choices you have more chances of avoiding burnout.

Watch out for the causes of burnout.

Action Plan

Do you see any of these attitudes or similar ones in yourself and/or list them down in your journal and write down your feelings about each of them.

DEAL WITH THE TWO SIDES OF BURNOUT

I'm not trying to work harder, just smarter.
—bumper sticker

How did I get over my burnout?

First, I had to deal with the *internal* causes.

I had to change my attitudes toward myself and my work. I was depending on my work to prop up a poor self-image. So I needed to heal that poor self-image. Now note that healing low self-worth and taming fears is a life-long process, but recognizing them within you is already a first step in the right direction. Remember that any addiction is a way of escaping feeling the most painful emotions of life. In this case, a burnout victim is using his work as the escape hatch so he won't feel the fears, the loneliness, the sadness, the traumas in his past. By entering into these feelings of pain, acknowledging them, embracing them, accepting them, and allowing yourself to feel their fiercest storms within will shrink these monsters to their true size.

A burnout victim doesn't genuinely love himself, and he needs to learn this *virtue* before he experiences healing. By allowing himself to feel his emotions *as is,* no matter how painful they are, he is giving a message to himself that "you're worthy" and "you're normal" and "I respect what you're going through."

Loving himself will also mean developing healthy boundaries between himself and his work and the people around him. Because the burnout victim has blurred his identity with the success or failure of his work and what other people say about him, he needs to distinguish his own worth from these two separate realities. He needs to learn that his life is *more* than his professional reputation and the bottom line of his financial statements. This "more" means his values or moral code and his spirituality. From this deeper self, he should then craft a higher purpose for living that is beyond career goals or financial objectives.

Finally, loving himself means adapting practical self-care habits—developing exercise, meditation, healthy diets, engaging hobbies, and other wonderful stuff that burnout victims and workaholics neglect.

Second, I also had to deal with the *external* causes.

My working environment was so awash with indecisiveness (mine) and the resultant disorganization, low morale, and chaos, was definitely a factor in my burnout. So for the first time in a long, long while, I faced my fears by meeting people I had conflicts with.

I made hard decisions at work, no matter how unpopular they were. I "created" a few enemies by doing what I believed was right. I removed staff who were hindering the mission of the organization. Believe me, healing my burnout wasn't popping a few pills into my mouth; it was major surgery!

I did this by asking help from people I could trust. Having a group of friends around, assisting and praying for me, was a real gift from God.

Finally, I determined that managing an office wasn't my primary gift. I was made to write and communicate, not run 70 people in three organizations. No wonder I was not enjoying my work! I decided to delegate the operations to those whose primary gift was management. It took more than three years and a lot of experimenting before I finally was able to turn over my jobs to others, but the whole exercise was worth it. I'm now more at peace.

Action Plan

Of the examples above, which can you apply to your life? Write them down.

What steps do you need to take which are not found above because they are peculiar to your situation? Write them down as well.

Who are the people and friends who can help you in your dealing with burnout?

DON'T BURN OUT; BURN UP!

> *The most powerful weapon on earth*
> *is the human soul on fire.*
> —*Ferdinand Foch*

After a bout with burnout, some people think that the way to go is to coast along and be boring. In other words, be monotonous so that you won't burn out again.

But that's not true. The antidote to burnout is to burn up!

Let me give you an illustration. Think of an oil lamp.

A burnout victim is simply a lighted oil lamp that didn't have oil. The result? The flame burned and consumed the entire wick rather quickly.

The solution is *not* to keep the oil lamp unlighted. It will not serve its purpose.

The solution is to *put oil* in the oil lamp and to light it again!

You and I were created for a purpose—for a sacred mission larger than ourselves. We need to live and be consumed by this higher vision!

But to be aflame by a vision for the *long term,* we need oil.

And that oil is *the core values written in the fabric of our soul.* We need to live by those values: love for self, for our neighbor and for our God.

And love for self will include the virtue of *balance.*

Because I don't need to borrow worth from my achievements as a crutch for my own self-value, I work in my job without the pressure. I work for love and the happiness that I feel in my work. There's balance! My oil is constantly replenished.

And when my day of departure comes, when my body reaches its end, I shall gladly allow the fire of my sacred mission to consume the last dregs of me.

Don't burn out; burn up!

Action Plan

If your job is "toxic," understand that no amount of changing the "system" will heal as much as if you first change your attitudes and behavior. Once you do that, changing the "system" will be much easier.

Do you have a sacred mission worth burning up for?

QUIT WORKAHOLIC HABITS

*I think you will find that if you arrange things so that
you find time to relax and "do nothing,"
you will get more done and have more fun doing it.*
— *Alan Lakein*

I was a true-blooded, full-fledged workaholic. I'm now converted and have become a lifeaholic — if there's such a thing. I'm now "addicted" to breath, to love, to quiet, to beauty, to balance, to peace, to joy, to simplicity and all the wonderful stuff contained in this adventure called life.

A workaholic works long hours.
A lifeaholic works regular hours.

A workaholic has very shallow friendships, in and out of work.
A lifeaholic treasures his deep friendships as his greatest wealth.

A workaholic works with no defined goals. He just wants to be busy.
But a lifeaholic has defined goals and works towards attaining them. And half of these goals have nothing to do with his work.

A workaholic has no interests outside of work.
A lifeaholic has pleasurable interests outside his work.

A workaholic cannot delegate.
A lifeaholic makes delegation his master skill.

A workaholic doesn't take vacations. And if he is forced to take one, his mind will still be trapped in his office desk no matter where he goes.

A lifeaholic takes afternoon naps, annual personal retreats, second honeymoons, regular family picnics and weekly days-off with gusto.

A workaholic feels that life is one huge problem.
A lifeaholic feels that life is one mysterious and wonderful gift.

The choice is yours.
Quit workaholic habits.

Action Plan

Ask yourself honestly: Are you a workaholic or a lifeaholic?

LAUGH MORE OFTEN

Angels can fly because they take themselves so lightly.
— Zen proverb

Laughter is one of the simplest, most inexpensive, drug-free stress-reduction gifts of the universe! Experience the healing energy of laughter flow through your body, soul and mind regularly. Simplicity means not taking yourself too seriously, and the alternative can only be laughter.

Norman Cousins, who pioneered scientific research on laughter, labeled laughter as "inner jogging," noting its healthful effects on muscle relaxation, heart rate and blood pressure. He writes, "I made the joyous discovery that ten minutes of genuine belly laughter had an anesthetic effect that would give me at least two hours of pain-free sleep." He credibly claims that his cancer was healed by laughter. And for him, his laughter regimen included watching old films of Laurel and Hardy and The Three Stooges!

Don't take life too seriously—especially the small irritations of your day. Instead of being frustrated at traffic, try laughing at the silly way we urbanites live.

Most especially, laugh at yourself and at your mistakes.

You might have seen this quote somewhere else (it's the stuff people forward to each other through e-mail) but I re-quote it here nonetheless because it points to what we've been talking about.

"If I had my life to live over...I would relax. I would be sillier than I have been in this trip. I know of a very few things I would take seriously. I would climb more mountains, swim more rivers and watch more sunsets... I would have more actual troubles and fewer imaginary ones... If I had my life to live over, I would ride more merry-go-rounds...pick more daisies."

Don't wait to live life over.

Do it now.

Laugh, or "jog," more often.

Action Plan

Do you laugh at yourself and the crazy things in your life?

Do you regularly involve yourself in playful activities? If you enjoy humor books and films, why not enjoy a good dose of belly laughter every once in a while?

Make a list of playful activities you want to try in the coming week.

LOVE YOURSELF

You shall love your neighbor as you love yourself.
—*Matthew 22:37*

Take time to care for yourself.

I used to think this was blasphemous. "How dare I think of myself?" I reasoned, "On the contrary, I should forget myself and focus on others and God!"

But Jesus took time to care for Himself, escaping to the sea or a mountain, away from the rush of crowds that wanted Him to meet their needs for healing, food and wisdom. He went home to friends (Mary and Martha and Lazarus) in Bethany when He wanted to rest for the night after preaching in Jerusalem for the entire day.

I believe that each of us have "love tanks" from where we scoop up and dispense love to others. If we keep on giving love to others, our love tanks will soon be empty—so we need to replenish that tank. In fact, when the hemorrhaging woman touched Jesus and got healed, Jesus said, "power had gone out of me." That was why He retreated into the arms of His Father and recharged and refilled His love tank.

After a tired day of speaking engagements, I know I need to refill my love tank. I switch into a "loving myself" mode by simply being quiet in prayer or having my wife cuddled up beside me or reading a good book or watching a good film.

Instead of taking the common vacations that people take these days (these vacations are so rushed, people come home wanting a vacation from their vacation!), I schedule "personal restoration retreats" regularly. These are very slow days of reading, walking, praying and a lot of sleeping.

Love yourself.

Action Plan

Are you comfortable with loving yourself? Why or why not?

List a few things you can do to love yourself this coming week.

EAT YOUR VEGETABLES

> *Our bodies are our gardens...*
> *our will are gardeners.*
> —William Shakespeare

I've been a semi-vegetarian for almost six years now. I eat fruits, vegetables and seafood, and I feel terrific. I'm not asking you to be a vegetarian, but I'm recommending that you simplify your eating habits. The rule is, *the closer the food is to its original form from the ground, the better.*

Every time food passes through a process of cooking, sterilizing, preparing, heating, washing or preserving, it loses its mineral and vitamin content.

Decrease your intake of *junk* food such as candy, alcohol, sodas and other stuff filled with refined sugars; and increase your intake of *real* food. Real food would include fresh vegetable salads. Make this a daily habit if you can.

You may not agree with their theology, but because Seventh-Day Adventists are mostly semi-vegetarians due to their religious laws, they have a lower incidence of breast, prostrate, pancreatic, bladder and ovarian cancer than the general population.

Can you hear your mother now?

Eat your vegetables.

Action Plan

How much processed and packaged food do you eat?

How much fresh vegetables and fruits do you eat?

Make a plan on how you can lessen the first type of food and increase the second in your personal or family diet.

CUT THE FAT

> *If you do what you've always done,*
> *You'll get what you've always gotten.*
> —Anonymous

How much animal fat are you eating?

High fat consumption has always been associated with heart attacks, diabetes, kidney disease, gallbladder attacks and premature aging. It's shocking to know that over 53% of people in large industrialized countries die of heart disease—and we all know that heart disease is commonly caused by fat deposits in our arteries. It has been proven that avoiding foods with saturated fat will also protect men from prostate cancer, which strikes over 25 million men each year.

Is it possible that God had our health in mind in this passage from Leviticus? "Speak unto the children of Israel, saying, Ye shall eat no manner of fat, of ox, of sheep, or of goat" (Leviticus 7:23). Read any health book today and they'll tell you what Leviticus recommended some four thousand years ago: Reduce your fat intake!

Reduce your fat intake by eating lean meat (i.e., chicken or beef; avoid pork altogether) only once a week—and eat more fruits and veggies!

Did you know that biblical Jews, historians say, ate meat only during festive occasions? It would be a great idea to imitate them.

Our health isn't the highest value. Love is, and we are willing to give up health if love demands that we sacrifice it. (That's why we have martyrs.) But normally, love demands that we care for our physical bodies and keep them in top shape so that we can excel in love, and love for a long, long time.

Let me say it again.

Cut the fat.

Action Plan

How much animal fat do you eat?

How can you avoid eating this? Try to learn to prepare more healthy food. There are a good number of cookbooks today that help homemakers cook delicious healthy stuff.

SLEEP WELL AND TAKE NAPS

In vain you rise early and stay up late, toiling for food to eat —
for he grants sleep to those he loves.
—Psalms 127:2

I think that we get into useless temptations to sin because we don't give in to our *legitimate* needs for rest, relaxation and recreation. I believe in that fully. We get tempted to impatience, irritability, laziness, lust, apathy, insensitivity—because we're just too tired.

Do you have enough sleep? Let me explain a little about the two phases of sleep: In the first hours of sleep, we have "deep sleep" which takes care of our *physical fatigue.* At the later part of our sleep, we have "dream sleep" (REM or Rapid Eye Movement sleep) which takes care of our *mental fatigue.* So if you cut short your sleep, you'll notice that your body may be handling the strain, but your mind and emotions and imagination are losing their sharpness and are craving for rest.

How much sleep do you need? This depends from person to person. Some can get by with six hours.

Others function well if they get nine hours. You'll have to find this out for yourself and this usually changes as we age.

If possible, take short siestas. According to Dr. Howard Clinebell in *Wellbeing,* there is scientific evidence that human beings may have the inherent tendency to take naps in the early afternoons. Researches have observed that nappers are 30% less likely to develop heart problems.

Good reason to sleep well and take naps, don't you think?

Action Plan

How many hours do you sleep at night? Do you feel this is enough? If not, what habits can you give up to increase your sleeping hours?

Is it possible for you to take short naps after lunch?

LISTEN TO YOUR BODY

The human body is the best picture
of the human soul.
—Ludwig Wittgenstein

I'm no jock. The truth is, I hate exercise. This goes
back to my grade school days when I looked like a
toothpick in my rubber shoes and couldn't even catch
a ball tossed to me from three feet away. In any sport I
joined, I managed to make the impossible happen—
like kicking the football straight into the goal—of the
other team. Or actually causing the basketball to fall
behind me when I tried to make a three-point shot.

But exercise I must, not because I've read it
somewhere in a book, but because I listen to my body
and "hear" it telling me, "I need some exercise. Take a
walk." And when I've overdone a particular exercise, I
"hear" it telling me, "That's enough. I need some rest
now."

Do you know that some marathoners and other
athletes are *more* susceptible to colds and other
infections? Because their bodies were telling them to
rest but they kept pushing nonetheless.

Respect your body, befriend it, and be keenly
sensitive to its quiet messages. When you grow in

intimacy with your body, you discover it to be very wise and communicative. It will tell you when it needs to sweat, when it needs to sleep, when it needs a bath, when it needs deep breathing.

Just listen to your body.

Action Plan

Close your eyes for a while and feel your body. What do you hear it telling you? If it's legal and moral and loving, why not do it?

GET SOME FORM OF EXERCISE

...while physical training is of some value...
—1 Timothy 4:8

All throughout my life, I made heroic attempts at jogging, swimming, weights and biking, and ended up martyred along the way. Before trying something, I'd get all hyped up. Like when I tried jogging, I went out and bought myself a cheap pair of running shoes, wrist bands, borrowed a timer's watch and even bought a jogging manual. That lasted for about two weeks, tops. The next time I jogged was three years later, and that only went on for one week. When I dove into swimming, I bought new trunks, goggles, and even ear plugs and nose plugs. They drowned after two weeks. (If you are practicing any of these or any other regular sport, I envy you. Keep it up!)

Like many people who watch TV-shopping networks, I got conned into buying an exercise machine that promised health and heaven in just three minutes a day. That lasted for a couple of months and I also conked out from that. It now sits in our storage room gathering dust, and surveys say that 95% of all exercise machines don't get used a month after their purchase. Ouch!

And then there were my trips to the gym that didn't last too long either. Thank God I didn't become a lifetime member — like my friend who paid a cool P25,000 for it. "What a deal!" he told me, "I can now go there forever and ever and ever!" He hasn't gone back there for five years now.

Today, I'm trying an exercise regimen called Earth Gym and so far, I like it. Perhaps it's made for athletically-challenged people like myself.

Randi Hacker in *How to Live Cheap, Green, and Happy* coined that term Earth Gym, as quoted in *The Simple Living Guide* by Janet Luhrs. In Earth Gym, there is no membership fee. And it is found right where you are. It's really simple: Look for patterns in your day or week where you could get exercise. A few examples?

There was a time when I lived on the fifth floor of an apartment building, so my Earth Gym consisted of walking up and down the stairs a number of times a day. To this day I also avoid elevators in any building I go to. And whenever I'm parking my car in a huge parking lot, I choose the farthest spot available from the main door so I can take an extra walk. No kidding! (I also save myself from the tension of competing with the other drivers who want the nearest parking spots.) During my weekly day off, I walk through a shopping mall back and forth to buy books and other stuff I need. Finally, my wife and I have our very important couple dialogues by taking walks after dinner. By doing that, we hit two birds with one stone: we strengthen our marriage and our bodies too.

Other suggestions by the Earth Gym proponents: make your house chores an exercise by not using electric vacuum cleaners and power lawnmowers, and go back to the basics of mopping, floor waxing and scrubbing. Walk or bike to and from your workplace.

Get physical.

Action Plan

Can you think of how you can include exercise in the daily routines of your life?

Discuss this with your spouse, children or other family members. Perhaps you can do some things together. This will help make you more faithful to your Earth Gym.

SIMPLIFY HOLIDAYS

By scaling down your activities,
You will have more time and peace of mind
to enjoy the ones that remain.
—Unplug the Christmas Machine

When my wife and I got married, we did the unthinkable—at least among Filipino nuptials: we had a potluck wedding reception.

We rented a huge basketball-court-cum-multi-purpose-hall beside the church and prepared buffet tables and lots of chairs. And our one thousand guests brought in the food! You should have seen the gigantic feast we had on that day.

Both of us had a good long discussion about it. If we were to do it the customary way, we'd have the reception in a hotel and pay the entire bill. But if we did that, we could afford only to invite two hundred guests. But we had more than two hundred friends! So we broke tradition and had a great time at our wedding reception. (Hosting an expensive wedding reception is such a burden for the newlyweds. I know of couples who even *borrow* money for this event. Can you imagine the catastrophe of starting your marriage with a debt?)

Christmas, New Year and Valentines are no different. We *can* break some customs if they weigh down our souls, rob us of our deep relationships and blow away our life savings.

- Should you spend a small fortune decorating your home for Christmas? Why should it be a competition as to who can have the biggest tree, the most lighted house, the most elaborate crèche, the most extravagant gifts… Can you decorate your home in a creative way that won't cost you a single cent? My family has been doing this ever since I can remember. We would even make our own Christmas trees with string, glue, thumbtacks and throwaway paper.

- Should you prepare so much food for so few people during parties? Why not do something different? For many Christmas Eves in the past, my friends and I would go around the streets looking for poor kids sleeping on the sidewalks. We'd give them food and greet them Merry Christmas a few hours before midnight.

- Should you really blow up expensive fireworks for New Year's Eve? How about holding a party for the poor instead? Or visiting a home for the elderly and giving each of them a gift. Ask your children to get their old toys, wrap

them up, and personally deliver them to a poor
family you know or to an orphanage nearby.

● Should you be so busy attending parties and
wrapping gifts that you have not even *one day*
to sit still and reflect on God's gift on
Christmas day? Perhaps you can take a break
on December 26. Go to a retreat house, a
convent or even a park. Spend a few hours
pondering on what transpired in the past year.
Pray and plan how you want the next year to
unfold.

Simplify holidays.

Action Plan

Is there a holiday approaching? How can you
celebrate it differently? Do some planning now.

154

BE AN ETERNAL STUDENT

I seem to have been only like a boy playing on the seashore and diverting myself now and then finding the smoother pebble or a prettier shell while the great ocean of truth lay all undiscovered before me.
—Isaac Newton

Take this exam and find out if you are an eternal student or not.

1. I try to learn one new thing a day.
2. I enjoy a sense of wonder; I am like a child when I am before something new.
3. I know I've got some talents that aren't fully developed yet and I'm taking steps to make them grow.
4. I love to read; I love to expand my intellect by reading from other fields and disciplines I know little about; I love to listen to good teachers; I wear down the doorsteps of the wise.
5. I always try to find new ways of expressing love.

6. I make it a point to listen to any person I meet, to enter his world and learn something about his life, be he a king or a beggar.

7. I'm adventurous when it comes to trying new things — as long as they're moral and healthy — such as eating new food, going to new places, dipping into new cultures.

8. I am open when my friends and mentors correct me. I admit when I am wrong, and have the ability to laugh at my mistakes.

9. I share my thoughts and opinions with joy and humility, knowing that I can be wrong and right at the same time. I'm not stubborn or obstinate.

10. I'm not ashamed to answer, "I don't know," when I really don't know. I'm not ashamed to also ask, "Will you teach me?"

Scored a ten? Heaven will be an exciting place for you, because there, we will keep on exploring and learning and growing.

Action Plan

What is one new thing you have always wanted to try but had no time to? Plan for it. Write it on your schedule.

What book will you read after you finish this one?

LET SMALL PROBLEMS REMAIN SMALL

> *Little things affect little minds.*
> — Benjamin Disraeli

I know of people who treat every little conflict, every little irritation, every little obstacle as a life-and-death emergency. I pity them. Because if we want to win in life, a master skill that we need to learn is the ability to let small problems remain small — and believe me, most of our problems *are* small.

One day, a friend of mine asked for help. He was working for a credit organization and wanted me to invest there so that he could earn a little from the commission of my investment. So I liked the interest rates he was giving me and dumped half of my life savings in his company. (At that time, I still didn't know *anything* about what I wrote in chapter 13 of this book.) Well one morning, I learned that his whole company collapsed and saw all my money disappear in a blink of an eye.

That was half of my net worth! Zapped to oblivion!

But I was amazed at my reaction. I sighed and shook my head and said, "Oh well, that's just money anyway." I walked home with peace in my heart and continued to live my happy life.

I could have done differently, you know. I could have blown up, focused on the negative and gone into depression. I could have panicked about my future, punished myself eternally with regret for not being more careful or stirred up resentment for that darn company. But I chose not to because life is beautiful. There were still so many things to be thankful for!

Has someone criticized you unfairly?

Did it rain during your outdoor party?

Has a friend taken you for granted?

Is the office air-conditioner conking out again?

Has another car just cut you in traffic?

Did your husband forget to fix the faucet?

Did the washing machine rip your favorite shirt?

You could decide to make a big issue out of it, use it to destroy your day, make it an excuse to be bitchy towards your family and allow it complicate your life.

Or you could choose the simple path.

The choice is really yours.

Let small problems remain small.

Action Plan

How do you react to problems? Try to think of a current problem now and then look at the bigger picture of life. Ask yourself: Will this problem matter 20 years from now?

SIMPLIFY AND LIVE THE GOOD LIFE

I went to the woods because I wished to live deliberately…
I wanted to live deep and suck all the marrow of life.
                    —Henry David Thoreau

Yesterday, I met an acquaintance at a shopping mall. He looked dashingly sharp. Cool shirt, stylish watch, Italian shoes. He was living the good life. Young women who passed by openly stared at him with gooey eyes. I bet if I did the *Lambada* right in front of them, they wouldn't have noticed me.

As an executive, my friend was earning oodles of money a year. Yet his news was mind-boggling: He was in debt, being buried alive. Credit card companies were after him, charging him for his high-spending lifestyle.

I couldn't believe my ears when he blurted it out. Mr. Oodles was borrowing money from me.

Me! The poor guy wearing a three-year old shirt, a pair of jeans worth P180 from Divisoria[1], and underwear that… never mind. I decided not to lend him, or I'd feed on his addiction. Instead, I told him to

---

[1]*A market for the masses, known for its cheap products.*

sell everything: his sleek car, his branded watch, his fancy gadgets at home. He told me he couldn't live without them. At that point, there was nothing else I could do but offer up a prayer.

That day, I went home feeling pity for the guy, but I also couldn't deny another part of me feeling very rich in my Divisoria jeans. I realized that though my lifestyle has been unbelievably simple, it has given me pleasure beyond measure. The pleasure of seeing beauty in the simplest things. The pleasure of being generous. The pleasure of being free.

And then it hit me.

It was *I* who was living the good life.

Ponder on it, my friend.

Simplify and live the good life.

Action Plan

Go through the pages of this book. Which chapters struck you most? Which do you feel you need to apply immediately to your life?

Do it.

A WORD FROM THE AUTHOR

Dear Reader,

My earnest desire is that this simple book enrich your life and refresh your soul.

If you wish to give me a message, my e-mail address is bomail@shepherdsvoice.com.ph. Because of the amount of mail we receive, I may not be able to respond to you. But I do promise to read your message.

We have a prayer hotline. If you have any prayer intentions, e-mail us at praybox@philonline.com.ph and we will be glad to pray for you. You can also write us at our head office, SHEPHERD'S VOICE, c/o praybox, #60 Chicago St., Cubao, 1109 Quezon City, Philippines, or call us at Tel. (02) 411-7874.

May you be firmly held in His grip forever.

I remain your friend,

Bo Sanchez

ACKNOWLEDGMENTS

To my forgiving spiritual family: the Light of Jesus, who had to endure the extremes their leader took them through in this journey of simplicity many years ago. Thank you for being patient with me.

To our devoted fulltime staff: you're God's gift to all of us.

To the energetic staff of Shepherd's Voice for making this book a reality.

To the big-hearted staff at ANAWIM who continue to live in simplicity for the sake of the poor.

To my children by acquisition who fill my heart with joy.

To the *lolas* and *lolos* and the sick in *ANAWIM,* who give us opportunities for love.

And to Marowe, for always being my best friend, and Benedict and Francis, for making Daddy smile.

BIBLIOGRAPHY

Carlson, Richard. *Don't Worry, Make Money.* New York: Hyperion, 1997.

_____. *Don't Sweat The Small Stuff...and it's all small stuff.* New York: Hyperion, 1997.

Clinebell, Howard. *Wellbeing.* Quezon City: Claretian, 1995.

Eyres, Linda and Richard Eyres. *Lifebalance.* New York: Fireside, 1987

Foster, Richard. *Freedom of Simplicity.* San Fransisco: Harper, 1981.

Jones, Laurie Beth. *The Path.* New York: Hyperion, 1996.

Luhrs, Janet. *The Simple Living Guide.* New York: Broadway Books, 1997.

Lynch, Peter and John Rothchild. *Learn to Earn.* New York: Fireside, 1995.

Sinetar, Maria. *Do What You Love, The Money Will Follow.* New York: Dell, 1987.

St. James, Elaine. *Simplify Your Life.* New York: Hyperion, 1994.

Stanely, Thomas and William Danko. *The Millionaires Next Door.* Longstree Press, Inc, 1999.

Yount, David. *Spiritual Simplicity.* New York: Simon and Schuster, 1997.

THEY NEED YOUR LOVE
Anawim: Refuge for the Poor

In June of 1996, *ANAWIM* began its full operations when an old man in dirty rags entered the bamboo gate of its rustic compound. The following week, a whole family of eight orphans arrived from the mountains. A few days later, a mother and her five children were running away from a physically abusive husband and father.

Four years later, the *ANAWIM* Center has become a refuge for 35 abandoned elderly, 10 poor children, two mentally handicapped persons, and countless of transients who seek inner healing.

Anawim, a Hebrew word meaning "the poor of the Lord," began with a simple dream of Bo Sanchez and the Light of Jesus Community. They wanted to love.

But giving love to the poor is costly. Feeding 60 persons each day — composed of the poor, the volunteers, the transients — is no small task. Medical bills are extremely expensive for the elderly. We spend P300,000 each month for this work of love.

Should you wish to help this work of love, contact or write to: ANAWIM, #56 Chicago St., Cubao, 1109 Quezon City Philippines. Telephone No. 725-8564. *They need your love.*

AN INVITATION TO KEEP ON GROWING

Should you wish to continue following the spiritual path explained in this book, you can read any of the inspiring publications of Shepherd's Voice or listen to the power-packed teaching tapes of Bo Sanchez and other speakers.

Check out our products online at www.shepherdsvoice.com.ph
or contact us:
SHEPHERD'S VOICE PUBLICATIONS, INC.
#60 Chicago St, Cubao
Quezon City 1109 Philippines
Tel. No. (632) 411-7874 to 77
Fax No. (632) 727-5615
e-mail: subs@shepherdsvoice.com.ph

ABOUT THE AUTHOR

Bo Sanchez is the founder of ANAWIM, a special ministry for the poor that provides a home for the abandoned elderly and a few children. He also established Shepherd's Voice Publications, a media ministry that publishes one of the most widely-read Catholic literature in the Philippines. He also founded the Light of Jesus Training Center, a teaching institute whose mission is to impart truth through seminars and workshops all over the country. He also established the Light of Jesus Community, an organization of lay Catholics from which was born the Light of Jesus Counseling Center, a dynamic group of volunteers who provide telephone counseling and other counseling services. Bo began preaching at the age of 13 and hasn't stopped ever since. He lives with his wife, Marowe, and sons Benedict and Francis in Manila, Philippines.

The #1 Inspirational Magazine in the Country

Bo Sanchez is the main writer of KERYGMA, the #1 Inspirational Magazine in the country. Get a whole year subscription of 12 exciting issues for only P500 . Feed your soul with God's Word at this affordable price!

Call us at (02) 411-78-76, or e-mail us at **sale@shepherdsvoice.com.ph**, or write to Shepherd's Voice, #60 Chicago St., Cubao, Quezon City 1109. Check out our website at **www.shepherdsvoice.com.ph**. or fillup the order form below.

Subscribe now! You'll be blessed 12 times a year!

ORDER FORM

Name: _____ B-day: _____

Address: _____

Telephone number(s): _____ Date sent: _____

E-mail address: _____

❏ Cash (Php 500 per subscription) ❏ Check ❏ Money Order

❏ Bank deposit thru Equitable PCIBank S/A No. 1280-00165-8
  (validated deposit slip enclosed)

❏ I am authorizing Equitable Card Network to charge my Visa/Mastercard
  in the amount of P_____

Card number: ☐☐☐☐ ☐☐☐☐ ☐☐☐☐ ☐☐☐☐

Expiry date: _____

Signature: _____

Last 3 digits at back of the card ☐☐☐

ORDERING IS EASY!
- By Fax : fax this form to 7275615 or 7269918
- By Mail: return this form with your payment (PMO or check payable to Shepherd's Voice)
    60 Chicago St., Cubao, Quezon City

Start your day right.
Every day.

Subscribe now!